NURTURING LITTLE READERS

A PARENT'S GUIDE TO EARLY EDUCATION

10 Easy Tips to Help Teach Your Child to Read and Write with Ease

KAREN FERNANDEZ

Copyright © 2024 by Karen J. Fernandez.

All rights reserved. No portion of this book may be reproduced in any form, stored in any retrieval system, or transmitted in any form by any means, including electronic, mechanical, photocopy, recording, or otherwise, without the prior permission in writing from the copyright owner, except as permitted by U.S. copyright law.

Cover and interior formatting by KUHN Design Group | kuhndesigngroup.com

First Edition 2024

ISBN 978-0-9894530-1-1 (paperback)
ISBN 978-0-9894530-2-8 (ebook)

Visit the author's website at www.abctraceandsay.com.

CONTENTS

Introduction 9

Tip One: Read Daily 11

Tip Two: Teach Songs and Poems 19

Tip Three: Teach Letter Sounds First 27

Tip Four: Teach Lowercase Letters First 35

Tip Five: Write Daily 41

Tip Six: Use Multisensory Learning Techniques to Teach 51

Tip Seven: Teach in Bite Size Bits 59

Tip Eight: Teach Words and Lots of Them 67

Tip Nine: Teach Small and Large Motor Skills 75

Tip Ten: Play Is the Work of Children 81

Resources 89

References 91

"Children are made readers on the laps of their parents."
EMILIE BUCHWALD

This book is for parents—the first and best teachers a child has. Parents know the intimate details of their toddler's life. What their child loves. What their child fears. Their child's strengths and weaknesses. Parents know when a child likes to play calmly and when their child is most energetic. They know when their child likes to cuddle and relax and when their child wants to be independent. Parents know a child's medical concerns and any limitations or modifications that a child might need. This knowledge matters and is essential to crafting a plan of learning unique to that child. This book is for parents who want to instill a love of reading, writing, and lifelong learning in their child.

INTRODUCTION

In most cases, we parents do not fear that our child won't learn to talk. We model daily, and often all day long, the skill of verbal communication. We praise every small attempt our children make at communicating with us. We brag over mumbles and gurgles and get excited over sounds like "da." All our excitement and goodwill trickles down to the child as they eagerly try harder and get better and better. And so, speech happens with little anxiety and little recognized effort on our part. Often, we have no idea how much modelling we do and encouragement we give daily to get our children to speak. Most of us teach our kids to talk all on our own, without the help of experts.

This can be done with reading as well. It *must* be done with reading as well. The foundations for reading are established by age five. That doesn't leave much time for a child to learn if you're waiting for preschool or kindergarten to begin. The process should start at home, well before school. And, like talking, reading can be taught over time, as seamless as teaching a child to talk. With the right attitude and a few simple tips, the process can be as easy and rewarding as helping your child learn to talk.

In these pages I will present ten research-based ways to get your child on the road to being a competent reader and writer. It's not a program you can buy; that comes later. This is about laying the foundation to make sure your child is ready for a reading program when they reach school-age, no matter what that formal reading program is or who is teaching it. Let's start the journey of helping your child *love* reading and writing.

TIP ONE

READ DAILY

"Reading is to the mind what exercise is to the body."
SIR RICHARD STEELE

It is not just quality time that matters when teaching reading; it is the amount of time as well. Reading is a skill learned over many years. Like riding a bike, you need more than a few high-quality lessons—you need time on the bike. That does not mean you are spending unpleasant hours trying to get your birth-to-age-five child to read. Quite the opposite. If done right, learning to read is fun and rewarding for both parent and child, and—like learning to talk—it is done during the daily minutiae of life. The most important thing you can do with your young child is make sure you read to your child each day. This is teaching. Read-aloud is fun and active instruction for the child and the parent. Reading is the most important subject in school because a child needs it to master the other subjects. How can a child answer questions or understand social studies in the higher grades if they cannot read the material? Generally, learning to read in formal school takes place from kindergarten to second grade. From third grade on, they are reading to learn.

Reading aloud to your infant helps them connect your voice and the book to comfort and security. Use primarily board books (board books are hard-back books for toddlers with no paper pages) with children up to age one. Babies like to mouth everything, and board books are a safe option. Feel free to give your child a teething ring or toy during this time so they learn not to chew on books. Never scold, because this must be enjoyable for them, and putting things in their mouths is normal behavior at this age. Keep the story to a minute or two. Use fun voices, never a monotone voice, to keep a child interested. For older children ages two to five years old, snuggling close for a story once or twice a day is great! Avoid long books when they are young. Pick books that are about topics your child enjoys. If the book is wordy and long and you are not enjoying it, the child probably won't enjoy it either. Shorter is better.

Have a shelf with ten to twelve books on it so your child is not overwhelmed with choice. Rotate your books as needed. Bring out books for each holiday or season. I liked to have a set time for reading. At night after bath was our time. Snuggled up in bed with nothing else to do was a perfect opportunity to captivate with a terrific book. Remember that the art of listening to a story must be taught and takes time. It does not happen overnight. Starting at birth and reading short, one-minute books builds listening skills.

Involve your child! Ask them to turn the pages. Let them conclude the book by learning the phrase "The end." While you are looking at the cover together, ask them what they think the book might be about. Invite them to say any repetitive phrases in the book. And be patient if they ask questions. They are trying to figure things out.

Always start by telling your child the title of the book, the author, and the illustrator. Explain to them what the author and illustrator do. This lets the child know a real person wrote this book. Often kids do not realize the story they read and loved was created by a person like them.

Reading the same book over and over to your child has numerous benefits. Repetition helps the child with understanding of the story. It builds their vocabulary, and they become familiar and comfortable with a great number of words. Repeat-reading will help the child to become a fluent reader (able to read quickly, accurately, and with expression) later. I memorized some books when my daughter was young, and yes at times it was tedious, but I knew the benefits.

Reading to your child from his or her birth to age five will start as a one- to two-minute activity, eventually extending to ten to fifteen minutes, and maybe longer. Many kids love to read for thirty to forty-five minutes a day. I always strived for two books a day.

Lastly, picture books are captivating for many kids. Children often sit alone with a book and concentrate deeply on the pictures, attempting to retell the story or just talking aloud to themselves while going through the book. I make it a point never to interrupt this time—they are on task, learning independently, and concentrating deeply. This is sacred time.

As you read, please use the journal pages at the end of each chapter to make notes about any information that is pertinent to your child.

This can help formulate a plan to incorporate the tips you value into your child's daily literacy routine.

Throughout this book, I'll be incorporating information from books and resources available via my website, The ABC Trace and Say Learning Center (www.abctraceandsay.com). You're welcome to explore these materials to aid you in instructing your child on reading skills. We firmly believe that every child can embark on their reading journey early at home, and who better to guide them than you!

NOTES ON MY CHILD'S PROGRESS

TIP TWO

TEACH SONGS AND POEMS

"Play is really the work of childhood."

FRED ROGERS

Some of the best purchases you can make when your child is young are a great nursery rhyme book and an awesome children's songs CD or playlist on a music-streaming service like Spotify. Here's why: Poems and songs support phonemic awareness.

Phonemic awareness is the ability to understand the sound structure in spoken words. Kids with good phonemic awareness can hear, identify, and manipulate the phonemes (letter sounds). Separating the spoken word *cat* into three specific phonemes, c/a/t, requires phonemic awareness. Why is this so important? Because a child's phonemic awareness is a strong predictor of their future reading and spelling achievement.

How do parents support phonemic awareness? By doing activities that help build sound skills. Just make sure the activities are quick and fun! Read books that have rhymes and short poems. Clap the syllables in familiar words. Help kids hear the beginning and ending sounds of words in a playful manner. For example, "Let's think of all the words that start with the letter sound /mmm/ like milk, mat, and mitten" and then say some silly and fun words that start with the sound *mmm*. Want a poetry suggestion? Jack Prelutsky has written some of the most loved children's poems. They are silly, whimsical, and engaging!

One of the best ways to teach phonemic awareness is through nursery rhymes. In fact, research shows that one of the best predictors of how well a kindergartener will learn to read is if he or she knows just eight nursery rhymes! Rhymes teach children how language works and help them to see and work with sounds within words. When children learn rhymes, they become aware that words sharing common sounds often share common letters. For example, the rhyming words *hat* and *mat* both end with *-at*.

Helping children master phonemic awareness sets them up for reading success and makes learning to read fun! I encourage parents to teach a short poem each month just by saying it with their child and adding hand and body movements. This takes less than a few minutes, and you can do it anywhere! While waiting in line at Target, while driving (save the movements for stop lights!), at lunch time, whenever. It's quick and easy, and the benefits are huge for the child. Play those children's songs and rhymes in the car. Your child will sing along and ask you to replay a song over and over! Once again, this repetition is beneficial.

I have a list of poems, songs, books, and other resources that support phonemic awareness on my website The ABC Trace and Say

Learning Center (www.abctraceandsay.com). Please don't hesitate to access them for support in preparing your child to become a reader. We're confident that every child can initiate their reading journey at home with parents as their guide!

NOTES ON MY CHILD'S PROGRESS

TIP THREE

TEACH LETTER SOUNDS FIRST

"Every child has a different learning style and pace. Each child is unique, not only capable of learning but also capable of succeeding."

ROBERT JOHN MEEHAN

So much learning takes place between a child's birth and age 5 that parents need to know solid teaching methods and what to teach to prepare their child for school. The goal is not to teach children to read before they start school, but rather to give them a literacy-rich early childhood as a solid foundation to support them when they are ready for a formal reading program.

Memorizing the alphabet song is not an especially useful skill for emergent readers, but **properly learning the sounds of the letters** does set children up for future reading success! Learning the letter sounds should come before learning the letter names because knowing the sounds allows children to read and write. Letter names are labels for the letters; they do not explain how the letters sound or how they are used within the English language. Therefore, the alphabet song is not so useful to a beginning reader.

Here are a few quick ways to help your child learn their letter sounds while keeping it fun, developmentally appropriate, and engaging:

- Instead of teaching the letter names and words, as in "*a* is for *apple*," teach your child letter sounds, as in "*aaa* is for *apple*." Letter sounds (the sounds that letters make) are learned first so we can read sooner. Letter names can be learned later.

- Instead of following ABC order, start with letters in your child's name. This brings more meaning and personal involvement to learning.

- Try not to teach visually similar letters together. For example, teaching letters *n* and *t* together is a better choice than *b* and *d* or *q* and *p*.

- Focus on teaching three to five new letter sounds a week. Your child will not remember all five in one week, but repeated exposure and review through play will cement their learning.

- Instead of old-fashioned drills, use multisensory learning to explore new letter sounds. Have your child trace letters in sand or on a tray with salt or sugar. Let your child paint letters with their little fingers. Have them use their whole arms to trace letters in the sky for a large motor activity and then have them trace on the carpet with their fingers for a small motor activity. One of my favorite activities is to pour a cup of pudding (store-bought is fast) on watercolor paper and have kids use their hands and fingers to draw letters. This involves seeing, touching, smelling, tasting, and hearing if you tell them the letter sounds as they play. Remember, children learn through doing!

Research shows that learning letter names will strengthen letter sound knowledge if introduced at the right time. So, when do we teach the names of the letters? Studies show letter names are best introduced after the child has learned the letter-sound correspondence. Letter-sound correspondence (matching the letter sound to the visual letter) allows young children to learn to spell, to write, and to read. If you teach letter names alongside letter sounds, you can confuse the beginning reader.

The *ABC Trace and Say Alphabet Book* can help your child easily learn the sounds that letters make and the correct way to form the letters. This can give your child an early advantage and set them up for success. Visit The ABC Trace and Say Learning Center (www.abctraceandsay.com) to learn more!

NOTES ON MY CHILD'S PROGRESS

TIP FOUR

TEACH LOWERCASE LETTERS FIRST

"What the hand does the mind remembers."

MARIA MONTESSORI

Many of us parents were taught to print our names in uppercase letters when we were young children, which meant we were taught the uppercase letters first. This confuses children because 95% of the written word is lowercase. When children look at books, most of the print is in lowercase. Teaching both uppercase and lowercase letters at the same time is too much. So, teach lowercase first because this will help prepare your child for the reading and writing process. The capitals can be introduced to your child later, as needed. Research now shows that children have a great advantage if they are taught lowercase letters first.

When teaching children to write their letters, the same logic applies. They will be writing most of their letters in lowercase, so teaching them lowercase letters from the beginning is less confusing and eliminates the need to re-teach later. Some people argue that uppercase letters are easier for young children to make because they are composed of mainly straight lines. But uppercase letter *E*, for example, uses four strokes, while the lowercase letter *e* can be made in one movement without a pencil lift.

ABC Trace and Say Alphabet Book helps children learn to make their lowercase letters by teaching them to use a continuous stroke font, meaning minimal pencil lifts. The book also breaks down the process of learning to write lowercase letters into bite-size, developmentally appropriate chunks for young learners. When children use this book to learn to make their letters, the parent is helping to train their child's brain using multisensory learning. The child begins by tracing letters with their fingers. Then, when they pick up a pencil or crayon to try to write a letter, they already know how to make that letter because they have done so repeatedly with their finger. The addition of the crayon or pencil is about learning to use the new "tool" to make the letter. A child can feel overwhelmed when they must learn to use a writing tool *and* learn to make a letter they don't yet know how to form. Break everything down into manageable chunks for them. Build their skills methodically and they will be successful. This will not happen overnight. As with teaching a child to talk, teaching a child to be a fluent reader and writer takes years.

ABC Trace and Say Alphabet Book is lowercase letters only. We know that correct teaching methods set students up to be successful. Visit us at The ABC Trace and Say Learning Center (www.abctraceandsay.com) to learn more about preparing your child to read and for a FREE lowercase letter-sound assessment sheet.

NOTES ON MY CHILD'S PROGRESS

TIP FIVE

WRITE DAILY

"Most lessons are learned through observation and experience."

RICHELLE E. GOODRICH

Learning to write can be an overwhelming task for a young child if the foundational elements of writing are not secure. I have watched young students be asked to write something in class and given a blank piece of paper on which to do it. For those who have the fundamentals down, this is a task they can begin and engage in. For those students who do not have the fundamentals down, this can be traumatizing. Why? Because there is so much to learn before age five about the writing process. They need to know that they start writing at the top and move from left to right on the page. They need to know how to hold a pencil or crayon. They need to know how to form some letters. They need some knowledge of letter-sound correspondence. They must be able to form an idea to write. A child who has had a literacy-rich environment will have some of these skills under his or her control and thus won't feel overwhelmed. They may write their name or attempt a word or two, maybe more. But a child who has none of these skills will be confused.

Writing is a necessity for daily life. It is a practical skill we all use to complete tasks. We make lists, fill out forms, send notes to people, etc. We must be able to write clearly and legibly to communicate and do our work. As a student, your child will be required to write by hand or on the computer so that teachers can assess what they have learned, and they need to be able to do so easily. We must write competently to communicate with others on a social level as well.

So how do you help your pre-age-five child prepare to be a writer? It starts with reading to them. All those board books you read to them from birth to about age two are going to help set those foundations in place because reading and writing support each other. The more your child reads and writes, the better they will be at both. When your child is around age two, you can help set the stage for success by adding in the small motor activities (see Tip Nine) to help their little fingers become strong. You can start using the *ABC Trace and Say Alphabet Book* at this point as well. This will help to cement the letter sounds and teach them to correctly form the letters. Our youngest learners must be able to write clear, well formed, legible letters. Research shows that handwriting is a foundational skill that supports reading, writing, and critical thinking. Consistently doing these three things with your child—reading aloud, teaching letter formation, and teaching letter sounds—gives your child a huge advantage in becoming a successful writer.

Next, you can add in time for your child to practice drawing, which, like the cave dwellers, is a child's first writing sample. Let them scribble away and use crayons, pencils, and paints! Have discussions with them as they do so, asking them what they are drawing. If they tell you a simple story about their drawing, write it down for them and make sure they see you write it. This is great modeling. My daughter would sometimes let me write her story on the front of her picture, but more often she preferred I put it on the back. I would ask her, "What is this you have drawn?" And she would say, "A dog and his house." I would say, "That's so fun. Look, I will write it for you now." And then I wrote it so she could watch and learn. If you write in front of your child often, they will start to make approximations of letters that may not look like much, but they will say, "I wrote *a dog and a house*." And you should say, "I love that you wrote that. How wonderful, you are writing too!" As we did when they were learning to talk, we praise all their attempts and model the behavior for them daily. We model then they attempt, over and over, getting closer and closer to the end goal. Again, do all of this with praise and great enthusiasm.

Modeling is important. Remember to explain what you are doing as you write. Your child does not know how your brain/thinking is operating, so you must be thorough in your modeling. For example, you can say:

> "I am going to write your story for you. *The cat is in the tree.* I will write *The* then leave a space, and next I will write the word *cat* then leave a space, and then I will write the word *is* and leave a space, and then I will write the word *in* and leave a space, and then I will write the word *the* and leave a space, and then I will write the last word

tree and put a period, which is this little dot at the end of the sentence that means we are done with that sentence. Now here is your story: *The cat is in the tree.*"

Point to each word as you read it. On the next lesson, use the same language. After a few times, pare it down to, "I will write *The* space, *cat* space, *is* space, *in* space, *the* space, *tree* and then the period." You could also just write the word *cat* for them and model it this way: "I will write the word *cat*. I will start with the sound *ccc*, the next sound is *aaa* and the last sound is *ttt*. That spells *cat*." If you do these small, five-minute or less writing lessons several times a week, your child will know what a word is and what a sentence is. They will know that sounds make up a word, they will understand spacing, they will know a period ends a sentence, and they will start to point to words as they read. WOW! The best first teaching is done by parents, in the home and on the fly during daily life.

You can also get a small whiteboard and dry erase markers and write one sentence a day for your child. Keep it simple. Sometimes I would do "I like" sentences for a week and ask my daughter what she liked and then write *Marie likes apples*. Or *Marie likes dogs*. And then she could draw the picture. Over time, she learned to write her name and then we shared the pen because she wanted to write her own name. This takes just a few minutes each day and helps kids understand what writing is and how it is done.

The writing process is a whole book unto itself, but these tips set your child up for future success.

Here are extra tips for parents that will help children ages four and up:

- Writing with your child and helping them is not cheating or copying, it is collaborating and modeling. Children need guidance when writing and help organizing their thoughts when they are young. This is how they become successful.

- Spelling is not perfect; it develops over time. Phonetic spelling is very appropriate at younger ages. Do work alongside your child to increase his or her spelling knowledge as they grow, but spelling should never hinder the writing process. It is a good idea to give the child a sight word list to keep nearby when the child writes. This list should have common sight words that cannot be sounded out, like *there, said, who,* and *the.* This way, your child practices writing the sight words correctly and eventually memorizes them. Good readers have memorized their sight words.

- Not every kid is going to be J. K. Rowling when they grow up. Not everyone excels at creative writing. That is why we teach informative writing, persuasive writing, descriptive writing, and narrative writing. They are all important. Your child could become a technical writer or business writer when he or she is an adult.

Never be afraid to model, help, or collaborate. When children learn to talk, we don't say things like, "They are just copying" or "They need to learn to do it by themselves." When teaching your child to write, never withhold your help or support. When adults are consistent in their modeling, collaboration, praise, and enthusiasm, children become great writers.

Always start on the star! *ABC Trace and Say Alphabet Book* has a star on every lowercase letter to show your child exactly where to begin when making each letter. This easy, interactive, tactile learning method will help you correctly teach your child with ease. Please check out the free tutorial video at The ABC Trace and Say Learning Center (www.abctraceandsay.com).

NOTES ON MY CHILD'S PROGRESS

TIP SIX

USE MULTISENSORY LEARNING TECHNIQUES TO TEACH

"All genuine learning is active, not passive."

MORTIMER ADLER

Multisensory learning is a powerful teaching tool. Using more than one sense creates stronger muscle memory for children. When we train the brain to learn a new skill and use multiple senses to do it (tasting, hearing, smelling, seeing, and feeling), we are helping students develop stronger memories around how to do it.

My daughter was four and in preschool when she brilliantly demonstrated this concept. She loved her preschool teachers, and they quickly took my place as the experts on how things were done. She could already write her name, and I had taught her the small letter *a* in her name. I used a continuous-stroke lowercase letter *a*, which can be made in one movement without lifting the pencil. We traced that letter in her name over and over, saying, "Around, up, down," and we traced it using sand, salt, and paint. It was an easy letter for her, and she wrote it effortlessly. She learned the letter over time and using multisensory techniques. But she came home after preschool one day and looked at me with her little hands on her hips and said, "We have been making letter *a* wrong." I said, "Really?" She replied, "Yes, my teacher said it is a circle and then a line." (They taught the ball-and-stick method where you make a circle and then lift the pencil and make a straight line down to create letter *a*.) I could see the challenge in my daughter's eyes. So, I replied, "She is right. You can make letter *a* both ways, and both are correct." I took a little wind out of her sails with that response, but she piped back at me with, "I'm gonna make it how my teacher says." To which I responded, "Okay, you can make it like that if you want." She *never* did. She had already been trained to make it the other way. It was cemented in her little brain and muscle memory is strong! That is why good first teaching is necessary. It is so much easier to take the time to teach the basics right the first time than it is to correct them.

Here are some easy and excellent multisensory activities:

- Create activities that you can easily pull out and use repeatedly. (When you create easy, ready to go, reusable activities you are more likely to get five multisensory lessons in a week.) Salt trays are the best! Pour salt on an old baking sheet and let your child trace shapes and letters and numbers in the salt. Then just store the small tray and pour the salt into a baggie to reuse next time.

- Playing with play dough, a great multisensory option. Laminate cards with lowercase letters and have your child shape the play dough into the letters on the cards.

- Sing! Songs are a wonderful way to incorporate multisensory learning. Many kids learn best from auditory activities.

Use Multisensory Learning Techniques to Teach

- Get moving! Learning through physical activity and body movement is key for young learners. Act out short books and poems. I keep these books in a box with props for them to use.

- Pudding on paint paper or plastic trays is also a fun multisensory activity. I like to use store-bought pudding, putting a couple of tablespoons on a tray so the child can make a few lowercase letters in it. This activity hits all five senses. They see the letter they are making, they smell the chocolate pudding as they are doing the lesson, they hear the letter sound when you say, "Make the letter *ssss*," they feel the way the letter is formed in the pudding, and they can taste the pudding right off their fingers. Wow! Using all their senses helps the brain maintain this new knowledge.

- Use *ABC Trace and Say Alphabet Book*. I created this book because some days I just could not get to a tactile activity, but I knew the importance of making sure my daughter knew the letters, the sounds the letters made, and how to form them correctly. So, I made a mock-up book and every day, from the time she was two until she was four, I pulled out that book for one to five minutes, tracing a letter or two with my daughter. After two years of spending just a minute to five minutes a day on this quick, easy, fun activity, she knew all her letter sounds and how to write her letters. I made it special, too. We started with a couple of the letters in her name and then we added more letters from her name. One day we made lemonade, and so I pulled out the book and we did letter sound *lll* as in *lemonade*. One day we did letter sound *aaa* as I cut up apple slices. Another day we did letter sound *ttt,* so I had her grab her favorite teddy bear to hold as we learned *ttt.* These extra connections to the real world help kids retain information. These were quick moments that sometimes I planned and sometimes were spontaneous. They were not long, drawn-out lessons. They were quick, informative, real-world, hands-on, fun lessons. This is how children learn.

NOTES ON MY CHILD'S PROGRESS

TIP SEVEN

TEACH IN BITE SIZE BITS

"I am always doing that which I cannot do in order that I may learn how to do it."

PABLO PICASSO

Most children do not remember learning to talk. They do not remember people modeling talking or the years spent learning to talk. It happened slowly over time and with little recognized effort. Learning to talk is broken down into bite-size chunks that children can easily manage, which prevents young learners from feeling overwhelmed and helps them retain information. That is also how to teach the reading and writing process—little by little, day by day, year by year. It is not a race. Unfortunately, not everyone knows the bite-size chunks to offer their child daily. This book teaches you how to offer a literacy-rich environment to your child daily in the form of play activities that will prepare them for a more formal reading and writing program.

When you break concepts or information into small chunks, you reduce the load on your child's cognitive memory. Basically, you make it easier for them. Bite-size learning is also great at this age because parents of littles are busy! Quick one to two-minute lessons throughout the day minimize distractions and interruptions. This creates a happy learning environment in which children thrive, with no pressure! Parents can set realistic goals for teaching a poem or a couple of letters and sounds, for reading a book or two daily, and for providing hands-on activities that lead to better learning results.

What do bite-size chunks of learning look like in real life? Parents of babies under age two should spend about two to ten minutes a day reading board books to their child, and they should build in lots of rich language while talking to the child throughout the day. For children between two and five, teach a poem or two monthly and recite it with them daily. Adding arm or hand movements to the poem expands the fun and the learning. In the car, play songs to promote singing along, which supports phonemic awareness. While preparing meals, offer time with play dough or a sand tray to support small motor development. Putting small finger food on the child's tray for the child to pick up also encourages small motor development. During the day, encourage your child to draw lines or circles in the sand or dirt with their fingers. Read a favorite book or two with them, allowing them to turn the pages—by age two or three many children should love sitting for ten to fifteen minutes for story time. You can break this time up into two reading sessions during the day if you like. Use the *ABC Trace and Say Alphabet Book* daily to teach your child how to form one or two new letters, and the sound the letters make. Have crayons and paper available for the child to draw, and then you can model how to write their name and/or a small sentence on their drawing. This is a lot of learning for a day! But it's all quick, fun, and engaging.

Lastly, parents are busy people. You don't have to do everything from scratch. You can buy play dough, pudding cups, a sand table for outside, and premade letter cards. I love to shop for Waldorf toys and Montessori educational toys also. Of course, you can use *ABC Trace and Say Alphabet Book*. Keep it simple for yourself and for your young learner.

More resources including a FREE Weekly *Activity Literacy Checklist* are available on my website, The ABC Trace and Say Learning Center (www.abctraceandsay.com). Feel free to access these materials any time to aid in your efforts to prepare your child to read. We firmly believe in giving every child an early start in their reading journey at home, and who better to serve as their instructor than you!

NOTES ON MY CHILD'S PROGRESS

TIP EIGHT

TEACH WORDS AND LOTS OF THEM

"There are many ways to enlarge your child's world. Love of books is the best of all."

JACQUELINE KENNEDY ONASSIS

The key to helping children read is words! Seeing words, hearing words, saying words, and using words every day. Just talking with your child guarantees them a larger vocabulary. A recent study found that young kids whose parents read them five books a day start kindergarten having heard close to 1.4 million more words than children who have not been read to. Wow! Does five books a day sound like a lot? Reading just one book a day means your child will hear close to 290,000 more words by age five than those children who are not read to regularly.

Big words come from books. Reading aloud to children broadens their vocabularies in ways that everyday conversations do not. In the children's picture book *The Elves and the Shoemaker* by Paul Galdone, the author introduces words like *garments*, *cobbler*, and *delight*. Rich language like this is common in picture books.

Point out interesting words when reading. One-on-one reading time with your child provides perfect opportunities to explain the meaning of larger vocabulary words. Point to it with your finger, say it, and then have your child say it. This is also a perfect time to explain to children that those funny shapes and lines (words) on the page mean something and create the story.

Take advantage of your child's interests. If your child likes dinosaurs, then find all the books you can about dinosaurs. What an amazing way to broaden your child's vocabulary! Words like *volcano, extinction, carnivore,* and *herbivore* are not words we use every day! Include fiction (made-up stories) and nonfiction (facts only) books, and books with illustrations and books with photos.

Read books *you* like, too! Your enthusiasm for the topic will be contagious. If you love astronomy, a picture book like *How to Catch a Star* by Oliver Jeffers would be a wonderful way to introduce your child to the subject and learn space vocabulary. Add a night of stargazing and a craft session of making stars from pipe cleaners, aluminum foil, or pretzels, and you will have some amazing hands-on learning right in your own home.

Once a child starts to recognize words, you can use index cards and a black marker to label some common items around the house. *Wall, window, cabinet, oven,* and *drawer* are some great ones for the kitchen. This helps a child understand that words can be written, and they represent things. The child can also start to pay attention to the beginning and ending sounds of words. This takes very little time but is excellent, interactive teaching.

For lists of fabulous read-aloud books, visit The ABC Trace and Say Learning Center (www.abctraceandsay.com). Reading to your child is teaching at its best.

NOTES ON MY CHILD'S PROGRESS

TIP NINE

TEACH SMALL AND LARGE MOTOR SKILLS

"Movement is the starting point for wiring the brain for learning."

GILL CONNELL

Building up the muscles in young children's wee fingers and hands can help develop small motor skills and make children confident writers. How do we build up these muscles and encourage a good tripod grasp, which is the ability to hold a pencil correctly? It is easier than you might think and can be taught through common playtime activities. Here are fun ways to help kids increase muscle strength in their hands and fingers:

- Put Cheerios or any other small cereal on the child's high chair tray or in a baggie, then encourage the child to hold onto each piece of cereal until they reach their mouth, building strength and hand-eye coordination. These are the same little fingers that will eventually hold a pencil.

- Finger painting develops small motor skills and hand-eye coordination. Children are learning to control their fingers when they finger paint, and their pictures are their first attempts at writing and storytelling.

- Beading is a great small motor activity that develops hand-eye coordination and strengthens small muscles. Beginners can manipulate large wooden beads and shoelaces. Smaller beads are better for older kids with more experience or stronger motor skills. Froot Loop necklaces are super fun and easy for beginners.

- Spray bottles strengthen hand muscles, thanks to the repetitive squeezing motion. Have children water your plants with a spray bottle. They can play with spray bottles in the bathtub or pool. Spray bottles are great for making pictures on the driveway!

- Play dough is an all-time favorite muscle-building activity. Plastic knives, cookie cutters, and a rolling pin are just a few tools kids can use with play dough. I love to make my own play dough, and often add spices like cinnamon for the holidays or a packet of Kool Aid for a fun smell and color.

- Tracing letters in the *ABC Trace and Say Alphabet Book* helps children develop hand-eye coordination while training their brain to make the letters correctly and easily. A two-minute lesson on letter sounds and letter formation each day will do it!

These are just a few ways to help small writers build up their hand and finger muscles. Digging in the dirt, planting, playing in sand, and sorting buttons into cups are a few more. Be creative and remember: "Play is the work of children."

NOTES ON MY CHILD'S PROGRESS

TIP TEN

PLAY IS THE WORK OF CHILDREN

"Play is the highest form of research."

ALBERT EINSTEIN

What should learning activities in the home look like for our youngest learners? Young children should be learning mostly through play, while older children should learn through project-based, hands-on learning. Did you know research shows that play is critical to a child's creativity and encourages divergent thinking? Play encourages young children to practice their vocabulary and grammar skills when they speak and try to understand others. Play that involves physical activities supports motor skills, strength, and endurance, which benefits physical and mental health. Play helps children learn to solve problems. Pretend play helps littles practice their future social roles, and trying out various roles encourages empathy and understanding. Play is the work of children and gives them the opportunity to practice what they are learning.

Scientists have learned that undirected play teaches children how to navigate small groups, how to share with others and how to resolve conflicts. Children who are active learners retain the information easier and faster. So, break out those board games, puzzles, crafts, and hands-on activities!

NURTURING LITTLE READERS

Reading activities that are play-based for littles could include the following:

- Magnetic letters on a cookie sheet or whiteboard to practice letter-sound recognition and sorting

- Salt trays for tracing letters and numbers

- Finger paints for learning to make letters and numbers

- Puppets or flannel boards to help children remember and understand stories by retelling them

- Books with matching dress-up clothes for acting out the story

- Play dough for making letters and numbers

- Tubs filled with crayons, markers, colored pencils, paper, and tape for making individual and personal books

- Small tubs filled with books that are themed—for example, books all about friendships for February

- A poem box that you add an easy new poem to each month for kids to learn

- Dot markers for making your child's name or for sight words

- Sorting games (laundry by color, buttons by shape or color, silverware, etc.)

- *ABC Trace and Say Alphabet Book*

Be sure to make PLAY a large part of your child's day.

It is important and rewarding to teach your child the foundational skills that will lead to the child becoming a reader and writer. You will set your child up to be an independent learner who can approach all subjects successfully. It is a long journey that takes years to perfect and cannot be rushed, but it can be a joyful and fun-filled journey that respects the child developmentally, especially when the parents are in charge. You know your child the best, so you can choose which letter sounds to focus on first, which books you know your child will love, which poems and songs will make your child belly laugh, and what activities will help him or her the most. Just remember, make it fun, teach through play, encourage small attempts, teach poems and songs, teach lowercase letters and letter sounds first, use multi-sensory learning, and read aloud to them. You got this!

NOTES ON MY CHILD'S PROGRESS

RESOURCES

ABCtraceandsay.com

Projectmontessori.com

Bellalunatoys.com

Lakeshorelearning.com

Discoverytoys.us

REFERENCES

Trelease, Jim. (2013) *The Read Aloud Handbook*. New York: Penguin Books

Willingham, Daniel T. (2015) *Raising Kids Who Read*. California: Jossey-Bass

From the editors of Teaching Young Children. (2015) *Learning About Language & Literacy in Preschool*. National Association for the Education of Young Children

Culham, Ruth. (2005) *6 + 1 Traits of Writing*. Oregon: Scholastic

Montessori, Maria. (2022) *Dr. Montessori's Own Handbook*. Read & Co. Books

McCarrier, Andrea et al. (2018) *Interactive Writing*. New Hampshire: Heinemann

Ginsburg, Kenneth R. MD. *The importance of Play in Promoting Healthy Child Development and Maintaining Strong Parent-Child Bonds*. American Academy of Pediatrics Publications, Vol.119. Issue 1, January 2007

Smith, Loren. *Finger Tracing Enhances Learning: Evidence for 100-Year-Old Practice.* The University of Sydney. September 2021

https://www.sydney.edu.au/news-opinion/news/2021/09/27/finger-tracing-enhances-learning--evidence-for-100-year-old-prac.html

Made in the USA
Columbia, SC
27 May 2024